TALES

FROM

GALILEE

Florence DeGroat

DeVorss & Company
P.O. Box 550
Marina del Rey, California 90291

Foreword

What a marvel it is that the stories of these Bible Events have come down to us with their vividness unimpaired and their importance undiminished! 2000 years of changing language and customs have only enhanced the great human interest which each Event portrays. Peter, John, Thomas, Mary, Martha and the Samaritan lady are our neighbors today; and their personalities are as clear to us as our own—maybe even clearer.

What could be better proof of the Oneness of the Human Race than the Power which these characters wield today? They help us to understand ourselves, our stumbling blocks, and the great Answers to Life's issues which are ours for the taking as soon as we are ready for them.

To read these inspired New Testament Events is a very deep psychiatric Treatment. They dramatize our own weaknesses and errors and successes by showing how they work out in 3-dimensional living. They prove the greatness of the Human Spirit, and the heroism of each struggling Individual as he or she approaches Spiritual Adulthood and is required to take up his Spiritual Birthright of Self-Awareness and Self-Responsibility.

They contain the Seed of the World-Resurrection which is taking place today.

Of course, the net result of this Race-Drama is to pin-point the unfailing Compassion of our Parent-Source, Who is fully aware of our most secret failings, but Who has forgiven them long before they appeared in planetary life.

Above all, perhaps, this New Testament Treasury shows that even the most deluded mortal is eventually courageous enough to capitulate and to implement his or her capitulation in decisive, constructive, *Universal* action. Even the hard-boiled Roman Centurion in charge of the Crucifixion was convinced of the Truth at last. Out of the darkness comes his redeeming cry, "Truly this Man *was* the Son of God."

TALES FROM GALILEE

*New Testament Stories
told in modern style
and linked up with
New Age Principles*

1

There was once a young girl named Judith who lived in the city of Nazareth in a country which is now called the Holy Land. Most of us know why it is called that, and as we go along with these stories we shall see again that the Spirit which walked there was indeed Holy. But, moreover, we shall see that the Person Who embodied that Spirit now walks the entire world and is the Answer to our own human, everyday, 20th-century problems.

It is mostly desert country in the Holy Land and the people have a very ancient history. Some of their kings and Prophets were very remarkable people, and they worshipped the *One God*, while most of the nations at that time thought there were a lot of gods. The One God of this Holy Land was *All-Good*. And He could do *anything;* while most of the nations' gods were not much better than ordinary people and they had very little power or desire to help or heal their people.

The people who lived in the Holy Land were called Jews. The founder of their nation was Abraham.

Judith was a very fine young lady. She was quiet and thoughtful and very lovely. She often walked around in the hills outside the city. Sometimes she met Someone Whom she called "The Man."

He, too, was quiet and seemed to be thinking. But he noticed her and loved her. She could tell that by His eyes. They were brown with gold in them. He spoke mostly with His eyes. They said, "I love you and I love everybody—even the ones who behave badly. In fact, that is why I have come to Earth—to help them to be really great people. They will learn this, and all is well. So let us be happy together today." He would sit on a stone and smile at her, and they were indeed very happy.

Later Judith sometimes wished she had asked Him more questions. But if she had, she might have missed the message from His eyes. After all, He had told her what she wanted to know. All is well; and God is indeed Good. God loves us and loves this Man especially. You could be sure of that. Life is forever, when we love each other. And forever means *forever*.

One Sabbath Day Judith noticed a great commotion around the Synagogue. Out came the Man and a great crowd after Him. They harried Him to the brow of a cliff and were going to shove Him over the edge. But they didn't somehow, and the crowd came back waving their arms and muttering, seemingly very disturbed.

Judith asked an old man what had happened.

"He claimed to be the Messiah," muttered the old man.

"What is that?"

"The Son of God. The One Who is to come and deliver us from all our troubles."

"Maybe He is," said Judith.

"Him? Ha! He's just Jesus—son of Mary and Joseph the carpenter. Brother of James and Joses. He's just got big *ideas.* That's all that's the matter with *him.*"

"Did they hurt Him?"

"No. He just sort of passed thru the midst of us and we saw him walking up a hill in the distance. Don't know how he did it. He wasn't even excited!"

"Why didn't His brothers protect Him, Granpa?"

"They're afraid to. Nobody can claim to be the Messiah around *here.* They'll kill him. That's what."

"Oh no they won't," said Judith. "That Man's a *Good* Man. He knows God. When I found a little bird with a broken wing He healed it—just like that."

"They'll get him tho. You'll see."

"Oh no they won't," Judith told him. And somehow deep in her heart she felt comforted and happy.

"He loves us," she said. "He loves everybody. And His eyes have a Promise in them. We'll see Him again—those who *want* to see Him."

"He's a trouble-maker," mumbled the old man. "But then again, I dunno. He does have a way with him. I saw him cure a mad dog once. We'll just wait and see what happens."

"Yes, you'll see," said Judith.

2

Simon Peter was my cousin. He was a great guy. Big and strong, but he never put on any airs. He was a lot wiser than I was too. But he didn't claim to be anything special. Just went about his fishing business with his brother Andrew on the shores of Lake Gennesaret here in Capernaum.

But one day a strange Man came along and called to Simon, who was in his boat with Andrew. I heard Simon say, "Lord, you'd better leave me. I'm not good enough." But he went, just the same. And Andrew went too. Simon was never the same again. That Man had a Power you wouldn't believe. And He was *Good*.

Anybody'd know that just from the way He looked at you. It said, "I've come to *help* you if you will accept Me." He changed Simon's name to Peter, which means "the rock."

I don't pretend to understand what happened. But I've heard tales and tales and tales, and they all hang together. The Man gathered up 12 followers and it seemed that Peter was quite important, although he never did *act* important. They travelled all over Palestine and tales of Wonder followed wherever they went. First the Man healed Simon Peter's mother-in-law of a fever. Then He changed water into wine at a wedding. Then He went up to Jerusalem and tangled with the big shots who claimed to know all about the Messiah. The more He quoted from their scriptures and did miracles to prove He was the Messiah, the more they hated Him and plotted against Him.

But He just went His way and walked over the whole country healing people and teaching the peasants. He seemed to love fishermen especially. James and John from our town were also His Disciples. But He

7

loved everybody. He knew already that there was one of His group who was waiting to sell Him out. And He knew that the officials resented His Spiritual Work and wanted Him to use His Power to get us free from Rome. But he wouldn't do that. Just minded His business and trained His Disciples to take over after He was gone. He knew which people were plotting to kill Him. Peter tried to tell Him not to go up to Jerusalem that last season. But Jesus was very displeased at that and told Peter that the Prophecies must be fulfilled and that He must die *and rise again*.

Nobody realized what He was talking about, although it is true the Scriptures say that the Messiah must be killed and rise again the third day. But He paid no attention to our babbling and just intentionally walked right into the trouble. His friend Judas Iscariot betrayed Him. The Chief Priests condemned Him and Pontius Pilate had to agree, because Pilate had been warned by Rome to keep the Priests pacified so there would be no general uprising. Pilate condemned Him in order to keep his job. But Pilate wrote over the cross when they executed Jesus: "Jesus of Nazareth, King of the Jews."

Well, Peter turned out to be a very great man. Even tho he denied Jesus the terrible night of His arrest, yet Jesus understood how deeply Peter regretted this and knew he would never do it again. Peter managed the Christian Church and the missionary work after Jesus was gone, and made a huge success of it in spite of the harrying he got from the authorities. Peter did really believe that Jesus had risen from the dead, and the power of that belief spread the Work over a lot of the Roman Empire.

I saw Peter once after the Crucifixion. Peter and his partners had been fishing all night and had caught nothing. In the early morning I heard Peter say, "IT IS THE LORD." He seemed to see Someone on shore. Peter hauled in a great draft of fishes after combing the sea all night for nothing. Then he jumped into the sea and swam to shore and was seen talking with Someone Who, they said, was Jesus, Who had risen from the dead.

Peter ended up in Rome and was finally crucified because he stuck to his belief and wouldn't take "no" from anybody. He was still the same old Peter who didn't think he amounted to much but was very glad to be able to die for what he believed.

3

It was my custom in those days to go up early in the morning to the Temple in Jerusalem to worship. As everyone in Palestine knows, the Temple was the Gift of King Solomon the Wise. Many years had the Temple been in building. And many centuries had the reverent feet of worshippers hallowed Its sacred walls.

Every inch of the Temple represented symbolically some Quality or Faculty of the One incorporeal, abstract, infinite God Whom we Jewish people worship. From the Holy of Holies to the Beautiful Gate, It speaks clearly of the God of Love, of Power, and of Beauty which has no limit.

Now this bright morning there stood in the Temple a young Man Whom all had heard of. From Galilee He came, and with Him tales of miracles performed, of Wisdom uttered, and of courageous rebukes aimed at those whose pious claims had proved shallow or insincere.

It seemed incredible that six feet of human frame could house so much vitality, dignity, purpose and Spiritual Thrust as His did at that moment. All eyes were upon Him as He made a small scourge of cords and looked with displeasure at the tables of money-changers and sellers of sacrificial doves which filled the Temple.

"Take these things away," He commanded, overturning the tables as He strode thru the Temple. "It is written in your Scriptures 'My House shall be called a House of Prayer.' But you have made It a den of thieves."

So much for materialism! He overturned the last table without a challenge; then calmly went about His business of teaching the multitudes.

In fact, it seemed that He preferred the multitudes to the Church officials. For His gentleness with fishermen and peasants was in sharp contrast to His scorn of unworthy authorities. Well He knew that the heckling which occurred at His meetings stemmed from those who should have been His supporters. But "The *common people* heard Him gladly."

And it was to a large extent thru the efforts of the "common people" that His Teaching spread far and wide and is now encircling the world.

4

I was just a lad in the days when Jesus used to come thru our town. His magnetism was felt far and wide so that word of His coming always reached us in due time.

This particular morning I managed to squeeze up thru the crowd to the front so that I could see what was going on. Down the road came a gentleman in a great hurry to reach Jesus. "My Daughter," he gasped. "On the point of death. Please, Master, come down with me and heal her."

Behind him puffed a servant." Your Daughter is dead," he reported. "Why trouble the Master any further?"

Jesus held the distraught father's eyes steadily. "Do not be afraid," He said. "Only *believe*."

14

They turned down a side road and I followed unobserved, altho I know that Jesus saw me as He always saw everything. At the gentleman's house, already the minstrels had struck up with their mourning music. When they saw Jesus, they performed more loudly.

"The maiden is not dead," said Jesus. "She is sleeping." At this a burst of scornful laughter followed Him into the bedroom, where He passed with the father and mother.

Next thing I knew the young girl was standing in the bedroom doorway *smiling*.

"Give her something to eat," said Jesus.

A bowl of hot broth was quickly brought, and I have never in all my life seen anything as beautiful as that young girl when the New Life began to flow thru her veins.

Someone closed the outer door with me outside; so that is the end of my story except that when I felt for my sore tooth which had been aching badly, I found that the ache was gone.

5

The Pool of Bethesda is a place of misery. I know, for I often come here hoping for my turn at the Healing which is said to take place when an Angel troubles the waters at times and the first person who steps into the pool is healed of whatever ails him.

There was a man who used to lie next to the spot where I usually sit. He had been diseased for 38 years and could not walk. What chance did he have to get into the pool before anyone else stepped down before him? Yet he had Faith that somehow, sometime, he would be healed. I used to laugh secretly at his persistence. But of course he had nothing better to do, so I supposed it didn't matter.

However, something happened one day which still has me pondering. Why did it happen to *him* and not *me*? Could it possibly be because he did have that long-time Faith while I had only *hope*? There is a tremendous difference between Faith and hope.

It was a very hot day and all of us around the pool were especially uncomfortable. What misery—to have to wait and wait, not knowing, but only hoping that *one* of us would be healed *if* the Angel should happen to come that day! It made us almost hate each other, whereas we should have comforted each other, seeing we were all in this negative condition together.

Seemingly out of nowhere, came a Man. He was well known to every resident of Galilee. He had been walking around the country for years, and they said He did miracles. Probably mostly folklore. People have to imagine *something* to give them hope for the future. The Man walked straight up to my neighbor and asked him,

17

"Do you wish to be made whole?" I felt that I knew the Man. He had something about Him which made you feel you had always known Him. My neighbor began his doleful story about how he couldn't walk and had no one to help him into the pool if the Angel should happen to come. Perhaps he hoped the Man would wait and help him when the time came.

The Man looked steadily at him and said, "Pick up your bed and *walk*." What a shock! My mind almost blanked out. What in the world did He mean? Yet His words were powerful—penetrating. Next thing I knew my neighbor was walking away with his bed. The Man returned to the group He was traveling with, so I had no chance to ask Him any questions. But then, there was something about Him which made people hesitate to waste His time. He seemed to have said everything already. He could see right thru you and know whether or not you were on the level with yourself and with God.

My neighbor never returned. I am sure he was really cured. Most of the others did not seem to notice that anything had happened. Too sunk in their own misery, I suppose. But I have done a lot of pondering about it. I feel that there is Good News in this Man's eyes. Sometime, somewhere, there will be Answers to all Life's miseries. And the Good which this Man brings is for *everybody*, not just for one person once in a while.

This Good isn't for me—quite yet. But the Scriptures say, ''Be assured the Kingdom of Heaven has come nigh unto you.'' I know that this Good is nearer to me since this happened. It is only a question of my being able to *believe* and *accept* It. And somehow, in the meantime, I do feel quite a lot better.

I have been told that Jesus found my former neighbor in the Temple after his Healing, and that Jesus said to him, ''Behold you are made whole. Sin no more lest a worse thing come to you.'' This gives food for thought as to the cause of disease!

6

A blind man sat by the roadside begging. This was no unusual sight, for he had sat there for years. This man had been born blind. Everybody knew him, and most were glad to contribute to his support when they were able to.

But today the blind man was very excited. Jesus of Nazareth was said to be passing that way. When he heard a crowd approaching, the man began to shout, "Lord, Lord, please help me." The crowd came closer. Friends tried to quiet the blind man. "Be quiet. Don't trouble the Master." But he cried yet louder. "Lord, Lord, help me—*please*."

Jesus stood still and asked that the man be brought to Him. "What do you wish me to do?" Jesus inquired. "Lord, that I might receive my sight," said the man bravely.

Jesus asked no medical questions. He spat on the ground and made a little clay with which He anointed the blind man's eyes. "Go and wash in the pool of Siloam," He told him. The man did so, and returned with perfect eyesight.

The crowd was stunned. "Is this the same man?" they asked. "I am he," answered the former blind man.

When the authorities heard of this Healing they summoned the man before them. "How is it that you now can see?" they asked him.

"A man named Jesus made clay and anointed my eyes and told me to wash in the pool of Siloam, and I now see clearly," he answered.

"Give God the praise," said the authorities. "We know that this man is a sinner."

"Whether he is a sinner or not I do not know," said the former blind man. "One thing I know. Whereas I was blind, now I see.''

The officials went round and round trying to make him deny what he knew had happened. ''Wherefore would you hear it again?'' asked the courageous man. ''Would you be His Disciples? Since the world began was it never heard of that anyone opened the eyes of one who was born blind? If this Man were not of God, He could do nothing.''

Making no headway with him, the authorities summoned his parents. ''Yes, he is our son,'' they testified. And ''Yes, he was born blind. But by what means he now sees we do not know.''

This conversation also went round and round, which was often the way when people debated about Jesus of Nazareth. Those who were healed *knew* what had happened and would not deny it. Those who were skeptical made no headway trying to discredit the Healer. Yet they did not dare to come out openly with their antagonism because the people loved Him greatly. This is how an undercurrent of antagonism gradually built up underneath the surface. Those who had no Faith became confused and resentful; and those who claimed to know all Truth did not wish to admit a higher Authority than their own traditional-minded selves.

Jesus, however, was working for the ages. He went His way, planting Spiritual Seeds in the Race Consciousness. Well He knew that the controversy must come to a climax at the appointed time. But he had been sent by our all-wise Spiritual Parent, so He knew He could win a global victory if He worked it as the Scriptures had decreed.

Plodding the dusty roads of Palestine was hard work. And coping with the antagonism of officials was still harder. But the ignorance of the people, He knew how to conquer. It was Love-in-Action which convinced the peasants and fishermen of the Truth.

For three years He planted Spiritual Seeds which He knew would one day sprout world-wide. He planted well and worked well; and when the time came to let antagonism have its way, He submitted with Grace and conquered the Race-error in the only way it could be conquered—by letting it come out into the open and be vanquished by the object-lesson of the Crucifixion and Resurrection.

7

Jesus travelled one day through the country of the Samaritans. The Jews and the Samaritans had an ancient feud, but Jesus paid no attention to it.

Towards noon He sat on a well and sent His Disciples into the town to buy food. They thought He was tired; but also it is probable that he knew there was a job here for Him to do. He could plant a Spiritual Seed in fertile Samaritan soil.

Presently—sure enough—a lady came to the well, a Samaritan lady. "Would you please give me a drink?" asked Jesus. The lady was astonished. "How is it that you, being a Jew, ask a favor from a Samaritan?"

she inquired. Jesus, as usual, ignored petty issues. "If you knew who I AM," He told her, "you would ask *me* for a drink and I would give you the Water of Life so that you would never be thirsty again."

The lady did not laugh. She said, "Sir, give me some of this Water." She had a glimmering of what He meant. He had been right. There was a possibility of planting a Seed with her. He astonished her by telling her that she had had five husbands and that the man she was now living with was not her husband. The lady was convinced that a Higher Power was in this Man. She hurried off to the town and told people, "There is a Man down by the well who knows everything I've ever done. Come and see Him. Isn't this the Messiah?"

When the Disciples returned, they were astonished that Jesus had been talking with a Samaritan. They pressed Him to eat some lunch. "I have meat to eat that you don't know about," Jesus told them. "My meat is to do the Will of my Father and to finish His Work." But the pious Disciples did not have the Spiritual insight which the

Samaritan lady had had. They did not perceive that Jesus referred to *Spiritual* Food. They asked each other, "Has anyone brought Him anything to eat?" So they showed themselves more material-minded than the Samaritan lady whom the Jews considered a semi-heathen.

So much for feuds based on bigotry!

8

I lived next door to Mary and Martha and Lazarus in Bethany. We were good friends, and Martha told me quite a lot about Jesus, who came to their house often for rest and privacy as He journeyed about the country.

Of course I did not interfere. But I knew Him well too. For once this Man looked at you deeply, you knew Him well and loved Him as He loved you.

His teaching was *different*. It was human, deep, and very much to the point. One time he came to dinner with Mary and Martha. Martha, who was a meticulous housekeeper, was running around, trying to honor Him with a lot of unnecessary detail. Martha was a trifle piqued because Mary spent her time sitting at Jesus' feet, listening to His explanations of Life. "Speak to Mary so that she will help me with the serving," Martha finally burst out.

But to her surprise, Jesus had a different idea. "Martha, Martha, you are careful and troubled about many things. Only one Thing is needful and Mary has chosen that better part, and it shall not be taken away from her."

From that day on, both Martha and Mary understood better the priorities of life and were more thoughtful women.

One time Lazarus became very ill. The sisters knew that Jesus loved Lazarus as well as themselves, and they sent someone to where He was Teaching to tell Him.

Jesus did not come, and Lazarus died and was buried. After a few days Jesus came, and both Mary and Martha assailed Him with "Lord, if You had been here, our brother would not have died."

"Where have you laid him?" Jesus asked. To His Disciples He said, " I am glad for your sakes that I was not here. It has happened this way so that you may *believe.*" Always He stressed *believing.*

At the grave Lazarus' friends were weeping wildly. Martha was the bravest. Usually she was the rock upon which they all depended. "I know," she said to Jesus, "that *even now,* whatsoever You will ask of God, God will give to You." A brave thought—and better than any of the rest of us could come up with! Jesus said, "Didn't I tell you that *if you would believe,* you should see the Glory of God?"

He was weeping Himself. But I think it was because we were all so defeated and He saw that after all, our Faith was very weak. Finally He looked up to Heaven and said, "Father, I thank You that You have heard me. And I know that You always hear me. But I said that because of the people—that they may know that You have sent me."

Martha at this point lost her courage. "Lord, it is too late. He has been dead four days!" she burst out. But Jesus called in a loud Voice, "LAZARUS COME FORTH."

And he did.

"Loose him and let him go," said Jesus. He meant that we should not only take off the gravesclothes from Lazarus, but also loose him from our own negative, binding *thoughts* of illness and death.

Jesus never minced words. The incident was over and He returned to normal living. But He knew that this thing He had done would travel around the world and remain a marvel for many centuries.

9

I am a physician. I am very much interested in the psychological aspect of Healing, and especially of the Healing of mental diseases.

I was in a position to observe carefully Jesus' technique in both physical and mental Healing (of both disease and psychosis). It is clear to me that He recognized a difference in these two classes of affliction.

With physical illness He usually addressed the patient directly with a positive command such as ''Lazarus, come forth,'' ''Maiden, I say unto you *arise*,'' ''Pick up your bed and *walk*'', ''Go, bathe in the pool of Siloam.'' Obviously, a positive impetus for the patient's will-to-life was needed. In one case He indicated that "Man, your sins are forgiven you" was tantamount to the positive command "Take up your bed and go to your house." So it is clear that the consciousness of wrong-doing (guilt-complex) may be the cause of the negative condition called disease or death.

But *mental* aberrations He handled in a different manner. As a rule He did not speak to mental patients directly. In the case of the young boy whose demon threw him into fits, Jesus dealt with the *father*. When He had established a positive contact with him, He addressed the demon directly: "Come out of him. And enter no more into him."

So it seems certain that in mental cases He diagnosed an exterior invading presence foreign to the Individuality of the patient. In other words, "possession." Afterwards He did not discuss the matter with the patient, but simply continued His usual practice of filling in with Spiritual Teaching wherever He saw an opening in the mind of man, woman or child.

The case of the *legion* of demons is especially illuminating. It seems that the point He was bringing out here was that violent insanity may be caused by bands of very destructive invading entities. "What is your name?" He enquired. "My name is Legion; for we are many," answered the demon.

This incident also brings out that demons have a certain psychic intelligence. They recognized Jesus' Spiritual Individuality and did not question His Authority. They asked if they could go into the herd of swine, and their violently destructive nature was evident from the insane action of the poor beasts, who immediately rushed into the sea and drowned themselves.

This gives us an idea of what a "madman" is up against. Only by our recognition of the psychic forces, and by applying the *Spiritual* (Universal) Truth, or Christ-Power, fearlessly to oppose them, can we rid the world of such psychic interference. This interference (and its counterparts in the various forms of common psychosis) is more prevalent than most people have any idea of.

10

That Man who comes around to our town once in a while, has more Power than anyone in all this world. People follow Him for days without even thinking how hungry they are or how tired they are either. He makes them feel so happy they don't worry about anything else. Even my baby brother will lie for hours in our mother's arms when He is with us. And usually Samuel is one restless baby—always wanting something or fussing about something. Looks as tho when the Man is here, Samuel has what he wants—whatever that is.

The greatest thing that ever happened to me was the time the Man came along and it was said He was going up into the mountains to give a lot of talks, telling us all about what God is like and how His own Power comes from God and that is how He is able to heal and help people.

An enormous crowd was with Him that day, and my mother and father just took off with them in spite of all the work they had to do. Somehow we didn't worry about the cow and the vineyard when He was with us.

We followed Him up into the hills, and when night came we just slept where we were. The baby loved it. And so did I. Finally we came to a clear space where there was a lot of grass. The Man found Himself a big stone to stand on so we could see Him, and began to talk. It didn't sound like a sermon, like at the Synagogue. It sounded just as tho He were talking to us in our own back yard—telling us what we had always wanted to know. We were all very happy.

"All the Law and the Prophets," said the Man, "hang on just these two Love-Commandments, which I will give you. (1) Thou shalt love the Lord thy God with all thy heart and with all thy soul and with all thy strength and with all thy mind. And (2)

Thou shalt love they neighbor as thyself. That's all. If you do that, then you are in line with God and will do right all your lives and be very happy.

"One more thing. The Kingdom of Heaven is *within* you. So you contact God mostly *within*. Live in the world and learn from what happens here. But your real Spiritual Life is within your own Be-ing. So you don't need to *lean* on anyone Spiritually except God. Prayer, Meditation, whatever you may call It, is our means of *growth*. So submit all you hear and see to your own Inner Guidance and *live* It no matter what other people may tell you to the contrary.

"Of course you can't love God," He said, "unless you know what God is and what is His-Her relationship to *you*. You can't love Someone completely unless you know all about what He's doing and why. It will take us forever to know God completely. But you'd better start right now because you can't live happily on this Earth unless you know the rules of living and agree with the Mind Which runs it.

"God is *not* just a Big Man. God is the Infinite, Universal Consciousness or Person Who includes *all of us*. God is *all that is*—the part you can see and the part you can't see. He-She-It is *Universal Spirit-Mind*. 'I AM Alpha and Omega—the first and the last,'—the inside and the outside. God is All and God is *All-Good*. And God is the Father-Mother of you and me, as He said, 'All of you are Sons and Daughters of the Most High.'

"You see God speaks thru His-Her Creation. He-She spoke thru the Prophets and that is why we study them. He-She speaks thru each of us as soon as we have grown up Spiritually so that we can understand Him. I myself am His Son and my Power comes from Him—*always*. Because I always do things that please Him, He loves me and shows me all His Mysteries. But the reason I always do what He likes is because I *want* to. I have learned that this is the only way I can enjoy life and use my talents.

"Everybody has talents, and we must find out what ours are and ask God whether or not what we *think* we want to do is part of His Purpose for us. If it is, then we can do it—beautifully—no matter what comes up to prevent us. But if what we think we want to do is *not* part of God's Plan, then we shall fail. So we have to learn to love God with all of our Be-ing so that we shall automatically *want* to do good and great things.

"The reason it always turns out that we *want* to follow God's Plan is because we are His Sons and Daughters, made out of His-Her very Essence, Which is *Universal Spirit-Mind.*

"Anything that is Life-Giving *for everybody* is from God. And anything that is selfish, or Life-blocking, is not. Isn't that simple? Just try it. Do something Good to help all the people in the world, and you will feel very happy and expanded, and you will have money enough for it without having to worry about it. But if you start thinking of *getting* instead of *giving*, or of puffing yourself up over other people, then your soul becomes smaller and smaller and you end up one unhappy, frustrated person.

That is what Earth-life is for—so you can try out your own ideas and find out whether they are selfish or Life-Giving.

"So you see that your whole well-being depends upon your loving God with all your heart (your emotions), and with all your soul (your Spiritual nature), and with all your strength (your body) and with all your mind (your reasoning ability). All of these must be balanced so that you can *grow*. For however great and fine we may think ourselves to be, there is always a lot more we must learn to be and to do so that we can keep on going ahead *forever*. Look at the stars. All of these are suns like our sun here. So there are that many worlds which belong to God, and we must learn to live happily on all these worlds. So you see there is plenty for us to learn and to do thru all Eternity.

"Of course you can't understand all of this right now. But if you will do as I say and love the Lord your God with all your heart, soul, mind and body, then you will *grow*. And when I see you again I can tell you a lot more so you can have the same

Power I have, from your Father and my Father, and from your God and my God.

"And if you do love God with all your Be-ing, you will also love your neighbor as yourself—not more and not less, but *as* yourself because he really *is* yourself. All of us are One *Within* the One and only God of our Be-ing."

"Who is my neighbor?" someone asked.

"There was once a man," Jesus answered, "who took a journey and fell among thieves. He was injured and stripped and he lay in the ditch, groaning. A Priest came along who thought he was very close to God. But he took one look at the poor man and shuddered and passed by on the other side of the road. Another man came down the road. He was a rich merchant. He also took one look and said, 'I must be about my business.' So he too passed by. Finally a Samaritan came by. Now you know the Jews think very little of the Samaritans. But this Samaritan took up the injured man and put him on his own ass and took him to an inn and paid for his keep and nursing until he got well again. He

41

promised to come back and pay more if it was necessary. Now, which of these three men was neighbor to the injured man?"

The crowd was silent. They got the point of the story.

There was a lot more talk which went over my head. But after 2 or 3 days Jesus said to His Disciples, "I don't want to send the people away without anything to eat. They might faint on the way home. What shall we do?" The Disciples were absolutely stumped. "We could never buy food for all these thousands of men, women and children," they said. Only Andrew had a helpful suggestion. "There is a lad here," he said, "who has a basket of fishes and bread." The other Disciples laughed and thought Andrew was silly. But Jesus took the fishes and bread and Blessed them and said, "Pass them around to the people."

The Disciples were still snickering a little but they passed them around, and what do you suppose? There was enough food for all those thousands of people! We all ate and gave thanks and had a wonderful Banquet sitting on the grass. When we had eaten all we could manage, Jesus said to His Disciples, ''Pick up what is left so that nothing is wasted.'' They did that, and there were 12 baskets full of leftovers! Where the baskets came from I don't know. And neither do I know how the crowd heard Jesus speaking in the open air. But they did. And I know that one reason Jesus saved the leftovers was so that we all would remember later that there was enough *and to spare* to satisfy *everybody*. He had us all sitting in companies of 100 so that no one could say later that only a few were there. There were thousands there.

This Banquet was because we had given up our ordinary work and come here to learn more about God Who is *everything* and Who has Plenty for *everybody* when we give up our own *hard way* and understand what God is and how we can work with Him.

That was the finest Party I ever expect to be at until I grow up Spiritually and learn to be like this Man Who has Power to be and do anything He wants to do; and what He wants to do is to help *all the people*. He helps us by showing us God.

They say the big shots hate Him and will kill Him. But they won't. You can't kill a Man like that. He will live forever, and as He said, He will come back and tell us a lot more as soon as we are ready for It.

11

I was a servant at the house in Jerusalem where Jesus ate His last supper. Of course every movement of this loved character stirred my deepest interest, and I made it my business as far as possible to find out what was going on. Little did I realize that I was to witness the most sublime and the most terrible night in history.

I hid outside the window and listened to the hymn-singing which accompanied the sacrificial Feast of the Passover. I could dimly see Jesus washing the feet of the Disciples and most lovingly instituting the Sacrament of the Bread and Wine. The

Discourse which accompanied this was far over my head, but intuitively I could feel the Heavenly vibration which emanated from the room. Of course I did not know that this Cosmic Event would be known as the Last Supper—the greatest utterance of Love-Wisdom ever spoken on this planet.

Early in the evening, one of the Disciples—Judas Iscariot—came out of the house and slunk down the alley where I was hiding. He seemed to be in a murderous mood, as indeed he must have been. But the exquisite vibrations from the group dissolved this unpleasant shock for me, and I followed happily when Jesus came out with His eleven Disciples and repaired to their favorite spot—the Garden of Gethsemane.

Jesus left His Disciples and went ahead to pray. What went on there I could not fathom. The happy evening had turned into a nightmare. Could the Master be in trouble? If so, it was as deep as the world and as dark as the pit. The Disciples were asleep.

Three times Jesus came back and tried to wake them, asking for Spiritual Help. But they were not capable of standing up to

46

what He was fighting, which must have been the grief and error of the entire Race.

The third time He said, "It is enough." And presently came a band of ruffians to arrest Him. This He obviously expected. Nor was He surprised to see Judas at their head, showing them the way. Judas betrayed Jesus *with a kiss*.

We followed to the Judgment Hall where the boasted civilization of Man fell into a thousand pieces. The farce which served as a "trial" was indeed the most lawless thing in history. Even Peter, the faithful one, denied his Lord in the terror of those hours. "I never knew the Man," said Peter. And then he went outside and wept bitterly.

The farce dragged into the sullen dawn of early morning. Pilate (unwillingly) ordered crucifixion. Mercifully, it was carried out at once, and the third act of the horror took place on the hill of Calvary.

Those hours I cannot recount. Such horror cannot be described. It seemed that the very Truth-Love-Life which constitutes Creation hung in the balance and could be snuffed out *unless* there was enough Faith in that *One Individual* to turn the Tide of Race Consciousness from death to Life.

The sun darkened. The Earth was heaving. Would everything collapse into chaos?

AT LAST thru the darkness came Jesus' Voice, calmly, confidently, "It is finished." At the same time came the voice of the Centurion in charge of the Crucifixion. "Truly, this Man *was* the Son of God," he said.

There *had* been enough of Faith-Love in this One Individual, plus an echo of that Faith in the mortal consciousness which had unwittingly slain the Truth, to serve as an axis to save the day for the Human Race! Since that dark hour, the Race has been travelling *upwards;* and seeming catastrophes are merely the outworking of this global Victory as It moves up thru the dark subconscious of Mankind.

12

I am Thomas. They call me "the doubter" because I could not share in the great joy of Resurrection morning. Yet I am one of the Lord's Disciples; and eventually I did recognize and accept the Truth of Jesus' global Overcoming.

As you may know, each Disciple of Jesus represents one of the 12 basic faculties of Man. Each faculty must be developed *and Christified* in each man or woman before Man as a whole can come into supremacy over himself.

The two women who first saw the Resurrected Lord came to us 11 Disciples and told the Story. I did not believe them.

That was because I represent the faculty of Man which needs to *prove* thngs in its own test tubes before it will accept them. You might call this the "scientific" faculty. The faculty of Imagination, the scientist does not trust. The faculty of Faith, he part-way trusts but as yet he does not know what it is he must put his Faith in. In his immature state he puts it in his test tubes instead of in the Unseen, Incorporeal, Abstract God Which is *Universal Spirit-Mind.*

That was the way with me before the Resurrection, or the New Age Consciousness, was born in me. But Jesus understood me and was patient with me; and later on He took pains to show me the scars in His hands and the deep wound where the Centurion thrust a spear into His side up under the heart. Jesus knows me deeply as He knows all, and He could see my Real Self underneath my doubting. Nevertheless, He said rather reprovingly, "Thomas, because you have *seen* you have believed. Blessed are those who have *not* seen and yet have believed."

In a moment I saw what He meant. If Faith, Imagination, and the other faculties were not able to perceive a *new* Principle (the Principle of *Spirit*) before It is proved in 3 dimensions, how would Mankind ever get off the ground? The caveman would never have progressed into the Man of Faith. And that was the way with a large part of the world before Jesus did His global Work and proved to us in 3 dimensions the absolute supremacy of *Spirit*.

This supremacy is, of course, what the physical scientist is frantically seeking. But it cannot be acquired from the *outside* inwards. Space limitation, body degeneration, all the fears and failures of 3-dimensional living, must be conquered by Man's *conscious* Unification with Universal Spirit. Spirit is *Causative* (Creative), and It automatically works downwards (outwards) thru Man to give him supremacy over what is called "matter" or Form. In other words, Spirit is Cause, and Form is the shadow of Spirit. Mankind is Individualized Spirit—the Son-Daughter of the Most High. He has dominion over his own lower vehicles and over the Animal, Vegetable and Mineral Life-Waves.

In the darkness of Gethsemane and

Calvary, the Race received a basic Correction. It saw that "evil" (or physical limitation) has no power to kill the Individual Spirit which has aligned Itself with the *Universal* Consciousness Which is God. Spirit, Which is Principle, and Which is dimensionless, is supreme over the objective Creation which It projects. And Mankind is Spirit, not "matter."

This is a tremendous lesson and I have not yet absorbed It completely. But tho I am slow to accept, yet by the very nature of my special faculty, when I do accept, I think things thru *scientifically*. The other faculties have something to learn from me also. And they will learn it as the Lesson of Calvary matures in the Race Consciousness. Most of us Disciples went to pieces and deserted in the shock of Jesus' arrest. So we see that all of us have much yet to learn about ourselves.

I see us all maturing as we assume the responsibility of carrying the Message to the unbelieving world. By our own experience in meeting other types of human mind than our own, we are each learning to balance our own 12 faculties and so to accomplish *our own* Resurrection. I see (clearly and scientifically) the New Day which is dawning. I see It spreading, maturing, and perfecting Itself in the consciousness of all types of people. I know that this will take many centuries. But I see in my budding Imagination faculty how the Truth is already spreading here in the Roman Empire and how It will be "preached to all nations" and finally (about 2000 years from now) how It will permeate all types of minds and show them how to fulfill their own Individualities while at the same time respecting the Individualities of all types of people besides themselves.

When my particular faculty has digested the Truth, it will contribute its quota to the Race development, in the "Scientific Age". BUT this faculty must learn to accept and balance the other 11 faculties in the Individualized Human Being Which is called "The Christ," and Which is the Reality of each of us and of the Whole of us.

13

Why did I do it? I have asked myself that question ten thousand times since the dark night when I (Judas) slunk out of the Feast of the Passover where Jesus was speaking His farewell words to His friends and preparing them for His departure. I could not stay there knowing that He knew I was the one who would betray Him.

The answer to my question, like all so-called "evil," does not make sense. I loved Him. I loved what He did to us. I loved the Truth and I loved the Work we were doing. But being an egotist I thought I could do it better. That was because I believed in material power and I saw that Jesus was refusing to build His World-Mission on that. Money! He could have had piles of money and formed an army to stamp evil from the world. Power! He had enough magnetism to enlist thousands and thousands and to build upon the great desire of the Jews to cast off Roman bondage.

On that triumphant day when He entered Jerusalem on an ass and the children strewed flowers in His path, we all expected Jesus to declare Himself on the side of material conquest. What a comedown when He dismissed the crowd and resumed His modest habits so that all that human material power was wasted! I determined right then that I was justified in betraying Him because He was bound to come to a bad end anyway. His reliance on Spiritual Power only was angering those who thought *they* were the purveyors of Spiritual Power. They would snuff Him out like a worn-out candle sooner or later, so I might as well have the 30 pieces of silver which my official friends offered me to betray Him.

Also—I must admit it—I was jealous. Such Power as He had! He had Power over the demons and Power over the elements and Power over the ethers and could produce something out of nothing to feed thousands! Why did He not make *me* His first assistant and let me manage the finances of His World-Movement? I had carried the bag for His group for years. But He did not seem to think that was very important.

So ran my tragic thoughts round and round after the night when I betrayed my friend and—I must admit it—my superior in material as well as Spiritual power. *He* did not have to scheme or betray for money. He could produce it out of the fish's mouth. I thought to stop these ghoulish memories by returning the 30 pieces of silver. Surely my official friends who had suggested the betrayal would reassure me that I had done right. But they took no pity on my remorse. "I have betrayed the innocent blood," I told them in anguish. "What is that to us? See thou to *that*", they sneered.

So I was an outlaw on both sides. I saw at last that the worldly power is neither glamorous nor secure, nor even loyal to its own. Surely they owed me some support. But they (as I had been) were supremely selfish and did not care what happened to anyone but themselves. Also—to be honest—they did not have any real comfort nor support to give. Each of them was living in his own hell as I am now and shall be until I straighten out my soul and find the true Security and the true Riches and the true, *Universal* Love.

What is torturing me is that I know I have already found them. But my demonic mania for worldly power did me out of allying myself with them. I knew the Truth as I walked the roads with Jesus and saw the Joy and Security in His eyes and its echo in the eyes of those who were helped by Him.

I hanged myself in order to get rid of the old person I used to be. But tho my body is gone, yet my thoughts remain. I am still alive. I still can feel and regret my own blindness. And yet—miraculously—I *am* still alive. And by this I know at last what Jesus was talking about. God is Life. And Mankind is the Son-Daughter of the Most High. Therefore we too are Life. Life cannot deny Itself. Everything that happens to us gives us *more* Life because by this we *learn*. Death is only the casting off of the old *wrongness*. Suicide is escapism. And yet by my death I did reject my old self-ness and set my soul free to accept the Good which I have seen and known and walked with.

It is not Jesus Whom I am afraid of. It is myself. For I know I must meet the same issue again in different form *and conquer it*. I have seen complete Compassion in Jesus' everyday doings and in His eyes as He looked at even me, knowing that I would betray Him. In fact, He knew all of Man's blindness and greed and jealousy. His Work here was just for that Purpose—to bring the issue into focus in 3 dimensions and to *prove* that Life, Truth and Love are victorious over the worst that egocentricity can do. He even said, "Those who are well do not need a physician; but those who are sick." And that means *me*. So His Work was for *me*.

I know that He forgave me before He was born here. And He forgave me on Calvary. What He wanted was that I (and others like me) should *see* the supremacy of Goodness, Forgiveness and of Aliveness for *all*. This I now see and I thank You, Lord.

14

Stephen was one of the sweetest characters in history.

He was very unassuming. You don't hear much about him in the Bible record. But when it came time for him to speak his piece, Stephen spoke it fearlessly and with complete understanding. He fully realized that holding to the Truth would be the cause of his death. And this he accepted with joy. He was perhaps the first martyr; but he did not think of it that way. He was just going Home to where the Lord had said, "I go to prepare a place for you."

After Jesus' Resurrection the authorities became alarmed. This "light-headed"

Christian Belief was tearing the hard-headed world apart. They took out after the Christians with a view to stamping out such nonsense in a hurry.

Stephen was haled before the authorities and questioned. He told them off in loving, but thoroughly competent terms. Out of their own Scriptures he recited the story of the age-long preparation for the Messiah, and tied in the prophecies conclusively with.what had just happened in Jerusalem. With the Authority of Spirit he proved his point and ended by citing scientific proof in the great Power which Jesus' actual Resurrection had evoked in the minds of the people of Palestine.

That Stephen was able to finish his discourse was proof of this very Power. For the wrath which kicked back at him landed him in the stoning pit. He took this as he took the court room. With perfect consistency he looked up and his face shone with radiance as he perceived the Lord and committed his Spirit into His hands.

The young man who took Stephen's

clothes as official witness to his death was named Saul. After his conversion, Paul rued this day. But by then he understood that Stephen's joy was sincere and that in very Truth "Death had been swallowed in Victory" for him as for the Lord Jesus.

15

The young man Saul of Tarsus was destined to become a power in the world for Good or evil. That mighty intellect and cast-iron will had to make an impact. For Saul was not one to hide his light under a bushel basket.

At first he enlisted on the side of retrogression. His learning, in the best tradition of the Pharisees, led him to reject the New Truth which had electrified the world-consciousness at Calvary and which was now struggling for a foothold in Palestine. Saul took responsibility for Stephen's death, and obtained from authorities permission to persecute the Christians, which he did, with great religiosity.

In fact it was on his journey to Damascus, where he intended to stamp out the Christian heresy, that Saul met more than his match in the Person of the Ascended Jesus. The Light of this Presence suddenly flashed in upon his darkened mind so that he fell from his camel and was blinded in his physical eyes. His reversal was immediate. "Lord, who art thou?" he enquired. Finding that it was Jesus and that Jesus fully understood his state of mind, he capitulated completely and permanently.

In Damascus, after several days, Saul was healed of his blindness, and was man enough to re-chart his life. Instead of persecuting Christians he now followed his Inner Voice and did his best to repair former cruelties and to further the Cause of world-Christianity.

Saul (re-christened by Jesus as Paul) was born for adventure. To avoid publicity, he was let down from the wall of Damascus in a basket by night in order to return to Jerusalem and try to reverse his unsavory reputation among the Christians there.

Jesus needed Paul. He was just the type to get the New Age of *Universal* Truth off the ground. But the smelting of the ore of Paul's Spiritual Gift did not take place easily. He went thru untold struggles and crises both with himself and with the world. The record of his missionary journeys reads like a spider-web of endeavor over the whole of Asia Minor and points beyond.

Paul was a *Universal* figure; and his efforts had to be prodigious in order to plant Seeds for global consumption. Because of his early reputation, he found himself in a questionable position with many Christians, in an out-and-out battle with his former traditonalist associates, and an unknown quantity to the rest of the world.

In spite of these heavy odds, however, he waged a fiery war for Truth and became a pivot to ray out New Age Principles to the nations. After one of his mighty crises with existing authorities, Paul uttered his New Age dictum, ''Lo, we turn to the Gentiles.'' He was known as the ''Apostle to the Gentiles,'' which really meant to the entire world population.

Paul's intellect was mighty. In at least

one court room he almost converted his accusers. His zeal was prodigious, and as he loved to recount later, he had been stoned, beaten, imprisoned, and generally reviled times without number in the great Cause to which he had now given his life. All this was necessary, however, in order to mold this volcanic nature into material which the Lord could use for the world-Purposes which He had in mind.

After many years of dynamic action, followed by imprisonment, Paul found himself on his way to Rome. Even this journey was fraught with near-disaster. The ship was wrecked and apparently saved only by Paul's Spiritual stature. On shore a viper came out of the campfire and fastened on Paul's hand. He shook it off and resumed his epic life-journey. In Rome he found himself a prisoner.

All in the web of his destiny, however. For it was from a Roman prison that the most influential letters of the ages were written by Paul to his fledgling Churches back home. So the troubled soul of this Apostle did finally succeed in sublimating his will-to-action from the destructive, bigoted level to the New Age level of Universal Love-Truth. At the end he was justifiably rather pleased with himself. ''I have fought the good fight.'' ''I have kept the Faith.'' ''I have finished my course.'' So he had. And his testimony is somewhat reminiscent of the Master's ''It is finished.''

Paul was finally executed—some say on the same day on which Simon Peter was crucified.

16

I (John) was quite young when Jesus called us from our fishing boats on the Sea of Galilee. We followed Him (brother James and I) and shall follow until Earth is perfected by the Love He planted in us and rolls up as a scroll giving way to another great Cycle in the Life-Experience of Man.

How we loved Him! Our old life was nothing and our new Life still unborn. The Thread which we followed was our Love for the Person Who personified all that we ever hoped to be, and Who knew us far better than we knew ourselves. He was here to show us what we are and how to become what He is—the Perfected Son of the Most High God. He summed up the Law and the Prophets plus His own Cosmic Teaching in His two Love-Commandments. ''Thou shalt love the Lord thy God with all thy heart and with all thy soul and with all thy strength and with all thy mind. And thou shalt love thy neighbor as thyself.''

Very early in the morning He would rise up and go to the hills. By a literal Mystic Process He renewed Himself there. Sometimes I followed in the hope of understanding how He did It. The dusty roads of yesterday, the heat, the crowds, the ignorance, filth and misery, fell from Him like an old coat and He came back radiant as the Reality is radiant, and ready to labor with us and the thousands who had enough glimmering of Light to cry to Him for Help and Life and Healing.

There were 12 of us Disciples chosen to be prisms thru which His Light should transform the world. Each of us represents a special faculty. My special faculty is Love.

It is the happiest faculty. But it needs the others to balance it. I especially need my brother James and he needs me. His special faculty is Discrimination. Love without Discrimination becomes sentimental and useless, while James without me would become stiff and harsh and negative.

What discussions and arguments we 12 had on those dusty roads! Jesus let us thrash it out in our own way between ourselves and learn from each other. He was not just a Teacher. He was an Educator. To educate means to "lead out." He drew out from the depths of our subconscious the elements of our Individuality. Even Judas Iscariot—the dark, brooding loner—had to work out his own neurosis in his own way in order to uncover his special faculty, which is Regenerated Life. After Judas hanged his *old* self, which was selfish and ingrown, Jesus was able to rise from the dead. A new man took Judas' place and the Age of the Resurrection was born. Judas himself has now fulfilled his own tragic destiny (self-created of course) and so has learned to love the Light, as he now does, better than he loved his *old* self.

Thomas! What a dissenter he always was! He is the scientist who has to prove things in his own test tube. How impatient we were with him! Even Jesus admonished him a bit. "Thomas, because you have *seen*, you have believed. Blessed are those who have *not* seen and yet have believed." But Thomas will fulfill himself. In that far-distant day 2000 years from now (which will be called the 20th century), Thomas will override the rest of us and dominate a great civilization. If the great World Plan is successful (and it will be), this will lead to Thomas' acceptance of Mystic Truth and to the harmonization of us 12 Disciples in a vibrant Age which will in turn introduce the very Kingdom of Heaven established on Earth.

So we followed—the 12 of us, stumbling, quarreling, denying, betraying. But always coming back to the Knowledge that this Ray of Glory was (and is) the only Hope of Earth. As Peter said in a moment of Illumination, "Thou art the Christ, the Son of the Living God." He was here! We knew It and we loved It! Peter's special faculty is Faith, and that is why he became the leader of the Work after Jesus ascended. Faith is the first-called Disciple, and all else is built upon that.

Each day had its special Glory. Those Healings! The lady who jostled her way to the front of the crowd to touch his Robe—and was Healed! The ten lepers, crying for Help, not daring to come too close but-finding themselves whole men as they walked! The little children Blessed and welcomed to the Feast of Love! The lady whose "sins were many" forgiven because she "loved much." The adulteress about to be stoned, forgiven but told to "Go and sin no more." The night on the sea when the storm stopped in mid-force! The coin in the fish's mouth! The draft of fishes on Easter Morning! Those blind men seeing, the crippled walking, the demons expelled! I could go on and on.

But always that dusty Figure ahead of us

led us on to *believe*, to *love* and to *understand*. To me the Guiding Light was Love. But I see now that I must also acquire and develop the other 11 faculties in order to attain full Resurrection of my Spirit, my soul, my mind and my body. That is why I am spending many years alone since my missionary work is done. Only thus can I understand what it was that Jesus found in the hills those nights when He battled with His Father within Him to slough off the tide of error which the world threw at Him each day.

The evening of the Last Supper! Some of them did not see what I saw. I saw the Personification of Love. I saw the dissolution of ego-separativeness and the dawn of Individuality which knows Itself but knows also Its One-ness with the All, and loves It *as Itself*. Jesus' Discourse that evening was liquid Love. But It was also Truth, without which Love is powerless.

It carried Him thru Gethsemane and 3 days of human hell. It brought Him to Resurrection Morning and to the Cosmic

Success which it will take thousands of years for the Race to assimilate. But It is with me forever; and like Sparks rising from a fire, I see more and more Souls waking to the great Glory which belongs to each of us and to the Whole of us. Amen.

17

I am a Christian girl living in Rome. My name is Claudia. I am in trouble with the Roman authorities because of my Belief.

In trouble? It is really just the other way around. I was never *out* of trouble before I learned this great Christian Way. And tho I think the authorities are after me and that I may be thrown to the lions in the morning, yet this is the first time in my life that I have ever really been at Peace.

You see, I was brought up to worship gods whom no sensible person could possibly believe in. They were worse than some of the people; and there was no telling really what they stood for nor what Life is all about.

I saw the most dreadful things. And nobody had any Answers as to why the gods allowed them to happen. Those slaves in the Roman galleys! They just sat there in their own filth and rowed and rowed until they died of disease and exhaustion. They hadn't done anything wrong except to get in the way of the Roman legions who wanted their land.

Then there were the spectacles in the arenas. People thrown to the lions and torn to pieces. And some of the Roman ladies *laughed*! Little did I think that I would be sitting here this night, expecting the same fate by daybreak. And still less did I know that I would be *happy* about it!

Whatever happens to me now is part of the great Rightness of the God of Love. If I go to the lions, then I am part of the great World-Awakening which will take thousands of years to break over the whole world. And if I go *gladly*, then that will be told as a witness to this marvelous Truth of the Goodness and Fatherhood of the One and Only God. This News will change the world into a place of Reason, of happy Accomplishment, and of Freedom for *everybody.*

Jesus told it all in Galilee. Also He *did it Himself.* The more you give *of yourself,* the more you receive. Isn't that simple? Because Jesus gave *everything* to the God Whom He knew surely to be the Essence of Love-Truth, He *received* everything. But what He cared most about was that one thing He received was the Power to give this Love-Truth to *anyone* who wanted It.

There are thousands already who do want It. And there will be millions and even billions more. At this time when death is so close to me, I have the vision to see the whole round world bathed in the Light of the very Truth. People won't know the world is round for a long time yet, but I can see it to-night. And roundness is the symbol for Infinity.

Good-bye false gods and cruel, ignorant beliefs. *All* people are Sons and Daughters of the Most High. And the Lord Christ

76

(Who is actually *One of us*) is our Way-show-er. He spoke It and acted It and gave It to us; and He is still helping us to understand and follow It.

I hear people shouting at the entrance to this catacomb where we are hiding. Farewell, dear friends. It is my turn to step into Eternity.

(signed) A follower of the Risen Lord